Rental Property Investing

The Ultimate Guide to Buying Your First Rental Property

Lawrence Anthony

Rental Property Investing
Copyright © 2018 by Lawrence Anthony

The contents of this book may not be reproduced, duplicated or transmitted without direct written permission from the author.

Under no circumstances will any legal responsibility or blame be held against the publisher for any reparation, damages, or monetary loss due to the information herein, either directly or indirectly.

Legal Notice:
This book is copyright protected. This is only for personal use. You cannot amend, distribute, sell, use, quote or paraphrase any part or the content of this book without the consent of the author.

Disclaimer Notice:
Please note the information contained within this document is for educational and entertainment purposes only. Every attempt has been made to provide accurate, up to date and reliable, complete information. No warranties of any kind are expressed or implied. Readers acknowledge that the author is not engaging in the rendering of legal, financial, medical or professional advice. The content of this book has been derived from various sources. Please consult a licensed professional before attempting any techniques outlined within this book.

By reading this document, the reader agrees that under no circumstances is the author responsible for any losses, direct or indirect, which are incurred as a result of the use of information contained within this document, including, but not limited to, —errors, omissions, or inaccuracies.

Printed in the United States of America

ISBN: 9781730710513

Dedication

- This book is dedicated to the individual who wants to be freed from the rat race of a nine to five job.

- This book is dedicated to the individual who wants to rent out a single-family house, townhouse, or condo and earn income.

- This book is dedicated to the individual who wants to experience financial freedom and work for themselves.

Free Bonus!

Simply as a "Thank you" for downloading this book, I would like to offer you a <u>rental property-purchasing checklist</u> to help you make a smooth transition into a successful investor.

For Instant Access Go To:
<u>http://eepurl.com/dO4TyD</u>

Also, I would like to offer you this free eBook called "Property Value Boost" to help you make the right decisions when investing in a property and becoming a landlord.

For Instant Access Go To:
http://eepurl.com/dPbQq9

Table of Contents

Introduction..8
Make Sure Investing Is For You............................15
Identify Your Investment Goals 21
Choose a Specific Real Estate Investing Strategy .24
Decide on Investment Type...................................29
Find the Right Market..33
Calculate Your Margins...41
Raise Cash for Your Down Payments 44
Begin Shopping For a Rental Property.................54
Build Your Team 60
Make Your Offer 74
Become a Landlord..78
The Different Landlord Hats 83
Operating As a Landlord 88
Tax Benefits of Being a Landlord 91
Compliance with Local,...93
State and Federal Laws 93
Landlord Insurance 96
Finding Tenants 101
Kinds of Advertising for......................................104
Renting Out Your Property..................................104
Screening Your Tenant Applicants......................107

Financial Background Checks 110
Turning Down an Applicant, Legally 116
Accepting Tenants 124
The Landlord-Tenant Relationship 126
Obligations and Responsibilities of the Tenant ... 134
Enforcing the Lease Contract 142
Hiring a Property Manager 154
Conclusion 164
Famous Quotes About Real Estate 166
CAN YOU DO ME A FAVOR? 172
Acknowledgments 173
ABOUT THE AUTHOR 174
NOTES 175

Introduction

First and foremost, I would like to thank you for purchasing this book "Rental Property Investing: The Ultimate Guide to Buying Your First Rental Property."

Do you want to increase your wealth with rental property investing? Of course, you do!

Do you want to learn more about rental property investing? Of course, you do!

Do you think a rental property is a suitable option for you? If the answer is yes, then this is the perfect book for you!

As a first-time investor, you will have a lot of queries, and this book has the answer to everything you want to know. But first, let me tell you how I got started.

How it all began…

I always wanted to start my own business, but I did not know in which industry. Initially, I wanted to become a personal trainer, so I thought naturally starting a business in the fitness and wellness industry was going to be my destination until I overheard a conversation at the gym. These two guys were talking about all the money they made in the last 12 months, and this was during the 2008/2009 economic recession. Right then and there, my interest in real estate was sparked!

After shopping around for a few months, in June 2009, I decided to purchase my first home in the city I love, Raleigh, North Carolina. I settled on a 1,300 square feet townhouse with two bedrooms, an open kitchen and living room, and a fenced-in backyard.

Before moving into my newly purchased townhouse, I used to live in a one-bedroom apartment with only two windows and a total of 640 square feet. My townhouse felt like a mansion to me because all of a sudden, I went from sleeping, eating, and living in 2 rooms to having more rooms than I needed. Nevertheless, my plan was not to live there forever. You see, I had set my sights on flipping houses and becoming a landlord, and in order to reach my dream of financial independence as quickly as possible, I had to purchase my first property. And that's exactly what I did.

Three weeks after the purchase of my home, I put 10 percent down on a brick ranch single-family home in Durham, North Carolina and turned it into my first rental property. Shortly after that, I converted my "starter home" into a second rental and purchased a larger home for myself.

I learned most of what I knew about finding and screening tenants, creating and signing leases, and managing my properties on several different websites. Some of the information was really good, and some were horrible and utterly false. To be totally honest with you, I made a lot of mistakes. Also, I never received family support because they thought I was foolish until they finally understood that, despite my lack real estate knowledge and lack of experience as a landlord, I was, in fact, making an enormous amount of passive income.

Fast forward almost ten years, and more than 25 properties in my portfolio, my financial independence dreams have come true. I have flipped more than 30 single-family homes and 80 percent of my rental properties have been paid off. Family members and friends who once thought I was crazy have changed their mind over the years. During the time of my writing this book, I make at least $27,000 per month in passive income, all the while, my tenants are actually paying off the properties with their money.

Here is what I wish I would have known

Still, it has not been a painless experience, and I made many mistakes along the way. And there are plenty of things I would do differently if I could. Unfortunately, it's true that some things need to be learned the hard way. This is why I am writing this book. I do not want you to make the same mistakes I did.

Therefore, in this book, you will learn everything you need to know about rental property investing. You will learn if rental property investing is a viable option for you, the different types of property that are available, steps to buy your first property, tips to become a good landlord, and much more.

Rental property investing is a great way to increase your cash flow. In the long run, with a little help, it can be a perfect source of passive income for you. Regardless of the reason for investing, you need to understand certain aspects of investing in a rental property, if you want to make a profit.

So, are you ready to get started? Then let us begin without further ado.

Part One

Make Sure Investing Is For You

Rental property investing does sound like a pretty straightforward concept, doesn't it? However, are you sure that it is the right option for you? Like with any other form of investment, even rental property investing has specific pros and cons. In this section, you will learn about the various benefits and slight difficulties you might face when you invest in a rental property.

Pros of Rental Property Investment

Direct income

The first benefit of investing in rental properties is the income you receive from the renters. It is an uninterrupted stream of income. The monthly checks you receive will directly go into your business account. For instance, if you rent a house for $1000 per month, you will earn $12,000 from the rent in one year. Okay, maybe that is slightly optimistic. Even if you expect just 75% in rents, you will still earn $9000 every year. That is a good source of income.

Passive income

If you hire a property manager to look after the property, the work you need to do will reduce drastically. You can earn money with little or no effort after a while. It is an excellent source of passive income.

Appreciation of property

Since you own the property, you stand to gain from any appreciation in the value of the property. Over time, the value of the property will increase. So, when you decide to sell, you can sell it for a profit.

Sweat equity

When you make any improvements to the property or upgrade it in any manner, it will add to the sweat equity. If you refurbish, repaint, or do some landscaping work, it will add value to the property. When the value of the property increases, the rent you charge can increase too. Increase in rent means an increase in your income.

Tax benefits

When you own a property, you can claim a couple of advantages and deductions. You can reduce the taxes you pay while your earnings increase. That's great news for all property owners.

Drawbacks

However, like with any form of investment, there are a couple of drawbacks to this form of investment. If you want to know whether rental property investment is the right option for you, then you need to be aware of the difficulties you might face.

Concentration of assets

Investment in rental property usually means that it will take up a significant portion of your assets. At least, that's the case for an average individual. The problem comes when there is no diversification of assets. If the investment doesn't provide a favorable return, you can lose your capital. However, you needn't worry about this. You will learn about different ways in which you can make sure that you make a wise investment in the coming chapters.

Tenant risk

If you find a good tenant, it is not an issue. However, if you find a troublesome tenant, you might find yourself in a sticky situation. What if the tenant doesn't pay the rent on time? What if the tenant destroys your property? Don't you worry about this? You will learn about the steps to vet your tenants and hire property managers who will manage these hassles for you.

Fees and insurance

There are certain insurances that you need to take your rental property. Not just that, the rental property needs to pass a couple of inspections as well. After all, you are the tenant, and you need to take good care of your property. The property taxes, homeowner association fees, and maintenance expenses might eat into your profits. Well, that's why you need an accountant to manage your taxes.

Active involvement

You need to devote some time and effort towards the maintenance and upkeep of the property. Some active participation is necessary. Even if you hire a property manager, you still need to keep an eye on the manager.

The risks involved in rental property investment aren't severe. A little due diligence and effort can easily rectify these drawbacks. The benefits it offers undoubtedly outweigh the negative aspects. So, do you think rental property investment is for you?

Identify Your Investment Goals

Now that you know that rental property investment is a good option for you, do you know why you want to invest? Without a purpose, you cannot get very far in life. The same applies to investments as well. Why do you want to invest? The reasons for investment will vary from one person to another.

Without a plan, the odds will not be in your favor. Without a goal and a plan to achieve that goal, the investment won't do you much good. Why do you need a goal? A goal will motivate you to keep going even in the face of adversities. When you have a goal, it is more likely that you will want to save for that goal. A purpose or a reason will help you to carefully think about the investment, returns, and the risks involved in the project.

The first step is to think about your goals. Do you want to invest to save for retirement? Do you want to build a nest egg for yourself or save for a rainy day? Do you want to save for your education? Do you want to buy a vacation home? Do you want to create a supplementary source of income? Do you want to leave a legacy for your heirs? Do you want to pay for a wedding? Do you want to start a business or donate? Do you want to secure your child's future? Do you want to secure your future? Do you want to attain the financial freedom to do what you want? Well, your reasons to invest can be any or all these reasons.

Congratulations! You know the reason for your investment. Now you need to arrange your goals according to the timeline. Goals can be short-term, mid-term, and long-term. For instance, a short-term goal is to save for an exotic vacation. An example of a mid-term goal is to save funds to start a business, to buy a vacation home, or even to save for your child's education. A long-term goal is to save for your retirement and so on. You get the idea, don't you? Don't make a list of these goals in your head. Make it a point to write all of this down. When you write your goals down and refer to the notes regularly, it will provide you the necessary motivation to keep going.

The next step is to decide how much each of these goals will cost. Attaching a dollar figure to some goals is easy. For instance, if you want to go to Greece for a week, you don't need more than $10,000. For other purposes, it might not be that easy. There are different online calculator tools that you can utilize to determine the specific amounts for the goals you set.

Choose a Specific Real Estate Investing Strategy

Well, you own rental property, and you might have a few questions. Like, what's next? What's your exit strategy? How will you be able to make money? Some real estate investors tend to buy rental properties with the aim of fixing them and then flipping them. Others tend to buy them so that they can have an excellent source of passive income, and others buy it with the intention of selling it later on when they need money. So, which way is the best way? Well, the answer is that there's no best way. The key is to know the type of investor that you want to be. Here are a few options that you can consider.

If you want to hold it for five years or less, then you should flip it. During the early 2000s, flipping houses was all the rage.

Flipping houses is a good strategy even today; however, it requires more patience. Flippers usually buy a property, make some improvements to it, and then sell it within a few months. The conservative or the part-time real estate investors who are intrigued by the idea of flipping usually have a five-year plan. They like to take things slowly and then make improvements to the property while renting it out and sell the property when it has appreciated in value.

There is no need to sell your property, even if the real estate market is red-hot at the moment. If you have got steady cash flow, then you don't have to sell the property; it can be a good source of passive income for you. You can also devalue the house for 27.5 years for lowering your taxes. Some people even hold onto the property until they can keep writing off the depreciation and when they can't do that, they tend to sell it.

The third strategy is holding onto the property and knowing that you will sell it when some event happens to trigger the sale. For instance, you might have a plan to sell the property when it's time for your child to go to college or probably for some other expenditure that you know you will incur in the future. Some people manage to sell off the property before it requires any significant repairs like a new roof. However, you probably will have to sell it at a lower price if you are selling a house that needs substantial repairs. However, in the meanwhile, you will be able to make use of it by renting it out.

If you are losing money on any property, you will probably want to get rid of it by selling it. Maybe the market has changed, and you aren't able to rent it out, perhaps the insurance or even the taxes have increased rapidly, and you won't be able to make any profit if you manage to sell it. Also if you are losing money, you might want to hold onto your property. Probably a new retail development is coming in the vicinity, and this will help in appreciating the price once again. There are a lot of things that you will need to consider, weigh in the variables like the loss that you are acquiring every month and also the reasonability of any positive change in the scenario in the future before you have decided to take a decision.

Let us assume that you are in the business and are expecting a good return on investment on your property. You have been holding onto the property for five years, and it has appreciated during this period. Therefore, you decide to hold onto it for a further period of five years in the hope that it will increase further. What do you do if it doesn't appreciate much in the second period? Before you start berating yourself for not selling the property when you had the opportunity, take a look at the rental income that you have been deriving it from it. Your ROI might not be significant at the moment, but at least it isn't vacant. You shouldn't stress even if you are holding onto negative equity in your rental property. If you don't have to sell it and can receive positive cash flow from the property, then you are fine. So, you can hold onto the property for as long as you will want to.

I am sure you know that there is no right answer to this question. No one can tell you for how long you should hold onto your rental property. If you do have a plan, then stick to it and don't let the fluctuations in the market scare you.

Decide on Investment Type

Now that you want to buy a rental property, you need to pick the type of property you want to buy. There are three main property types to choose from, and these are single-unit residential property, a multi-unit property, and commercial real estate.

Single-unit residential properties

The best option for a first-time rental property investor is a single-unit residential property. These often cost less and don't need much maintenance when compared to the other options. You can buy a single-family home. It doesn't have any shared walls, and it is constructed in a single lot. It has square footage than condos or townhouses. They usually have a front or a backyard. Since you are the owner, you will be responsible for all the costs of maintenance. They tend to attract long-term renters who are financially stable. The resale value of such units is high too. The next option is to buy a condo or a condominium. They are single units within a large complex or community, with shared walls. It might offer different amenities like gym, clubhouse, and a pool. Since you are the condo owner, you will be a part of the homeowner or the condo owner's association and will need to pay a monthly fee. The costs of maintenance are low when compared to a single-unit residential property. The third option is a townhouse. A townhouse is a cross between a single-family home and a condo. They tend to have shared walls with other units next door. It is significantly larger than a condo but doesn't afford the privacy of a single-unit home.

Multi-unit residential property

It usually consists of two to six units that an investor purchases as an investment. A typical situation is where the owner owns the entire building. The owner might live in one unit and rent the other portions, or even rent all the portions. The maintenance cost is higher than the different property types. However, they have a higher potential for positive cash flow.

Commercial real estate

Typically, an experienced investor will want to invest in a commercial real estate. It is a great technique to diversify investments. You can rent the space for commercial purposes. Since it is for commercial use, the rent you can charge is higher. With this type of investment, you can have a mix of residential and commercial units. However, it needs a commercial mortgage.

What kinds of property are you interested in purchasing?

_____

_____

_____

What are the pros and cons?

Pros

_____

_____

_____

_____

Cons

_____

_____

_____

Find the Right Market

When you look for a rental property, here are a couple of things that you need to keep in mind.

Neighborhood

The neighborhood you select will determine the rent and the kind of tenants you can attract. The quality of an area also influences the price of the property. For instance, if you buy a rental property near a university, your tenants will most likely be students. Also, make sure that you know the neighborhood regulations about rentals before you decide to invest.

Property taxes

Property taxes aren't fixed, and they vary from one region to another. You will pay the property tax from your pocket. So, make sure that they aren't too high. If the taxes you need to pay are high, the rent will be higher, and it might make it difficult to attract tenants.

<u>Schools</u>

If you choose to buy a family accommodation, then you must consider the educational facilities in the neighborhood. If you want your potential tenants to be families, then the proximity to educational institutions is a parameter you must consider.

<u>Crime</u>

Who wants to live in a neighborhood with a high crime rate? You can obtain the crime statistics from the local police station or public library. Look at the rates of vandalism, burglaries, petty crimes, and thefts before you invest.

Job market

A location with excellent employment opportunities will attract more people. Not just that, it also helps to increase the value of the property. If a new company or an industry is bound to come up in the location you favor, the number of potential tenants you can attract will increase.

Amenities

If there are malls, hospitals, movie theaters, gyms, and markets within a two to a four-mile radius of the property, you can attract renters. It all comes down to the comfort of the renters. If essential amenities are available nearby, it makes the property infinitely more attractive.

Future development

If there is scope for future development, then it is always good. An area with a reasonable growth rate means better facilities for the renters.

Listings and vacancies

Check the available listings and vacancies in the neighborhood. If the vacancy rate is high, then you must avoid that area. There must be a reason why tenants don't prefer a specific area. It doesn't make sense to invest your hard-earned money into an investment with no potential tenants. The idea to invest is to earn money and don't forget this fundamental point.

Rents

Check for the existing rental rates as well. Rental income is your reason to invest, and you need to be aware of the average price in the area. If the rent isn't anywhere close to the costs you will incur, then it is not a good investment. You can talk to other homeowners and real estate agents to get these numbers.

Natural disasters

Insurance is an expense that you must never ignore. It is an expense that you will deduct from your earnings. In an area that's prone to natural disasters like floods, cyclones, or earthquakes, the insurance amounts are quite high.

Always keep your goals in mind

Investors need to know the reason why they had entered the rental market and what is it that they wanted to accomplish. If the goal was to earn passive income and live off it, then you will need to make provisions for various tax provisions as well as deductions. For instance, you can deduct depreciation from your taxable income.

Get your finances in order

Being aware of your income and expenses will help you in securing additional loans for buying more property. Don't forget to include various costs like insurance, maintenance, management, utilities provided, major repairs, and taxes as well. Talking to financers and mortgage brokers will help you in buying property with as little money as you possibly can. For instance, first-time homeowners can buy an apartment building which can accommodate four-units, then secure a Federal Housing Administration loan with a 3.5% down payment, collect the security deposit and then make use of the rent that you receive towards the down payment.

Always keep your options open

Consider investing in smaller markets that exist within the secondary markets, the construction of the house and also the rent that people are paying in the general area. Before making a purchase, you should see how well the house was constructed, the potential tenants, and the additions that you can make to the property for increasing the rent. You won't be bringing in a new demographic, but you should make specific changes to the existing property in such a manner that the current tenants won't mind paying a little extra for it.

Steer clear of low-interest rates

If a property is about years old and if it will cost a high amount to build a new one, then you shouldn't buy it. Make sure that the property has got enough value to get reasonable returns when you want to sell it in the future.

Renovations

Renovating the kitchen and the bathroom can help you in getting a higher rent. Making sure that the fixtures and fittings are of good quality and are modern, this will help in raking in higher rent, but make sure that the cost of the renovations doesn't exceed the income that you are planning to make of it.

Always screen the tenants

It is critical that you screen your tenants before you let them in. Have a detailed application process and check for any criminal or civil lawsuits that they were involved in, their credit scores and so on. You will need a tenant who isn't troublesome and also promptly pays the rent.

Calculate Your Margins

You can increase your wealth and net worth with rental property investing. In fact, it is a great way to rake in money. Now, you need to calculate your margins so that you can determine whether the property is a right investment decision or not. So, how do you figure your margins? How much rent should you charge? Will the method of down payment you opt for change your calculations? Earning money is a numbers game, and you need to get these numbers right.

When you calculate the expected rate of return on a property, make sure that you take into consideration the different costs that you will incur when you own a property. Think about how these costs will affect your bottom line. The rate of return is an essential consideration, and you should never skip this step. For instance, when you decide to invest in equities, you will expect a rate of return of 5% to 8% annually, won't you? So, what is the rate of return that you want? Do you expect that rate to grow every year or you happy with a constant yield?

Keep in mind the opportunity costs when you buy a rental property. You can pay for a rental in two ways. You can either take a mortgage for it or pay it with cash. It might sound like quite a stretch for an investor who is just starting out, but you need to take this into account. If you decide to pay for the property with cash, what is the opportunity cost involved? A significant chunk of your capital will be in the form of cash that you cannot use for anything else. If you purchase a home with $100,000 in full cash, you will at least expect an annual return of 6%. It means that you expect a monthly profit of about $500 from the investment. Regardless of your mode of finance, you need to make sure that the property you invest in will yield the kind of returns that you are looking for.

Raise Cash for Your Down Payments

The most straightforward manner in which you can make use of less cash for buying rental properties is opting for houses that are cheaper. The market prices are majorly responsible for determining the price of any rental property. You needn't have to spend all your money on acquiring a rental property. You can buy something for a lower price and then spruce it up if you feel like it. You can also purchase rental property as an owner-occupant. It means that you can live in that property for about a year or so and then you can rent it out. This technique does help you in saving a lot of cash. However, the payments you make towards interests on loans and mortgages will be higher. The higher fees tend to hinder the cash flow from these investments.

Buying a multi-family property unit is another owner-occupant strategy. If you have managed to buy a property, which has about four portions, then you can get a bank to sanction an owner occupant loan on it, provided you reside on the property. If you want to, you can rent that unit out after the completion of one year. You can also reduce the amount of cash that is required for purchasing a rental property by opting for seller financing.

The one problem with seller financing is finding a seller who is willing to give you the necessary credit. The cost of seller financing might be higher than your regular bank loan. You can also partner with another investor. It means that the amount you are investing in it will reduce considerably and you will still be able to share in on the profits and take the decisions as well. However, make sure that you have got an agreement in place so that there won't be any unnecessary disputes later on. An extremely risky strategy is to buy a rental property by taking out a hard money loan and then refinancing that property into a traditional mortgage. However, for executing this strategy, you will need to have a lot of experience, and it is quite risky.

The most straightforward manner in which you will be able to save money for investing is by directly saving a portion of your income. You can save up to 50% of your income for the sake of investment. It isn't precisely easy regardless of the amount you earn every month. Our society, as well as the economy, has been designed in such a manner that it is easy to spend and challenging to save money. If you manage to keep your spending habits under control, then you will be able to save more money. It doesn't mean that you shouldn't spend or that you should live frugally. It means that you should go about sensibly spending your money.

Saving your tax refunds

You can always save up your tax refunds for making a future investment. It isn't difficult. You can set up your bank account in such a manner that the minute you receive the check for the tax refunds, it is directly deposited in your savings account. It will help in making sure that you haven't spent this amount on anything unnecessary.

Setting aside a portion of your paychecks for investing

You can talk to your employer and get them to set aside a part of your monthly paycheck to invest. If you are self-employed, then you can direct your bank to set aside a portion of your monthly earnings for investing in real estate. They will need to withhold a certain percentage of your monthly income. Depending on your comfort level, you can decide this percentage. It can be as high or as low as you want it to be.

Living frugally

If you are interested in investing in the real estate market, then you will undoubtedly need a lot of funds. You can do this by living frugally for a while. Living frugally doesn't mean that you need to take on a Spartan existence. For a while, you can prioritize your expenses. You can postpone any expenditure that seems unnecessary or ostentatious for a while. Maybe you want to purchase a pair of Louis Vuitton pumps; this can certainly be put on hold for a while. You will be surprised at the amount of money you have been able to save by merely prioritizing your expenses.

Whatever isn't a necessity can be indeed postponed.

Home Equity Lines on Primary Residence

There are different reasons for which you might want to get a HELOC (home equity line of credit) like for refurbishing the house, any home improvements or even for investing in real estate properties. Setting up a HELOC isn't expensive, and it costs a fraction of the amount of credit that you are looking for. You might not need the money immediately; however, it does come in handy when a great investment opportunity comes along your way.

The qualifications that you will need to fulfill for getting a HELOC are quite similar to the ones that you will have to meet for getting a regular mortgage. The bank will require you to have a good credit score and an income that can help to back up the amount for which you are seeking a loan. The requirements for all this will differ from one bank to another and also on your loan requirements. You will need to have equity in the property you hold. The capital is the difference in the value of your property and what you owe against that property. Banks have got different ratios for the loan, and value and this depends on the type of property you hold (whether it is an investment or a personal residence).

The variable rate on the home equity line of credit is around 2% above Wall Street Journal- prime rate and the flooring rate is set at 5% while the ceiling rate is 21%. You won't be charged any monthly or any yearly fees and will only have to pay interest on the money that you have made use of from the HELOC.

The bank will need to get the property appraised, and once that is done, after paying a few fees the HELOC will be granted. With this form of credit, you get the option of paying off the debt at any time that you feel like.

Most of the conventional banks offer HELOC as well. However, it is wise to check the charges that are levied on such line of credit. Make sure that you are reading all the documents related to this scheme carefully before taking a decision.

Side jobs/businesses for extra cash that you use towards purchasing rental property

You can start your own business. When you have got a business of your own, then you have all the control, and the opportunities for making more money are high as well.

Holding and maintaining rental properties can be a business as well. You will need to make sure that you are running the business and it isn't the other way around.

The business should be able to make money for you without much hassle. The most straightforward manner in which you can get more money is by just asking for it. If you are working for someone else and you know that you are doing a good job, you can directly ask for a raise. If you think you don't have a reason for asking for an increase in pay, then in such a case work harder so that you can ask for what you deserve.

If you think that you have reached a saturation point in your current employment, then you can consider changing your career. You can shift to something that you genuinely enjoy and like doing. It is never too late to do something you love. There are different ways in which you can make more money for yourself by doing something you like. There are various options out there, and you can engage in any of these if you want to earn an excellent income on the side. You can make use of this income for investing in real estate properties.

Begin Shopping For a Rental Property

Fix and flips

It is also known as a fixer-upper and is for investors who are looking for an active source of income from short-term investments. In the fixer-upper method, properties are acquired, renovated, and then sold. Don't think of it, as a quick scheme that will make you rich, but when you do it correctly, then the investor will profit from this particular strategy. When you are looking for a property to fix and flip, then it is imperative to analyze all the deal-breakers.

Once you have set a budget, you should probably consult an inspector, then a contractor, and an appraiser as well for identifying any potential issues regarding time and money that's involved. Time is the most prominent asset when it comes to flipping.

The longer it takes to flip a property, the more expensive it will be. The benefits of this strategy are that the competition in the market is slightly less. Not many people want to get their hands into a fixer-upper. So, you don't have to worry about a lot of competition. It does cost less than a ready-to-move-in house. Not just that, you have complete autonomy with regards to redesign.

Many risks are associated with the fix and flip strategy. Therefore, you will need to remember that your goal, in this case, is quite simple and it is to make money. You won't be able to afford any budget blowouts, because it will slash down your profits.

The main risk that you will face is a situation wherein you can buy a property, renovate and then not able to sell it for a profit or unable to sell it. The other risk is spending more on the acquisition of the property, then spending some more on renovating it. The result will be an expensive property that might be too costly for that particular market.

You need to be realistic about your profit margins if you want to avoid the risk of over-capitalization. You probably won't be lucky to sell a house for $1 million in a reasonably priced neighborhood, where a property can be sold for about $350,000, and prime property is valued at around $500,000. If your plan for renovation is something complex, then you should seek out the help of an expert builder who will help you in this process. It can make a difference between your success and failure. Therefore, think carefully before deciding about the renovations that you want to undertake.

Make sure that your purchase contract includes a condition for pest inspection as well. The building and pest inspection will help in identifying any significant defects that can help you in reducing the price during negotiations. Also, make sure that you have sought the approval of any local council for beginning your renovation.

There's no denying the simple truth that the expenses of getting in and out of investing in property are quite a deterrent for many buyers.

Expenses include stamp duty, the commission of the agent, advertising, any legal fees, mortgage costs, and any other costs incurred in this process need to be factored into the project budget. Your profit is the sale price minus all the expenses incurred in renovating the property, the costs, and the purchase price. Spend some time calculating the costs of entry and exit that are involved in every property that you are interested in purchasing. It will help you in making up your mind about a particular property and its viability.

Low-cost homes

The option that you should consider when you decide to invest in rental property is a low-cost home. You can enter the retail market without spending hundreds of thousands of dollars. Unless you live in a vast urban area, it is quite likely that the houses in your city will fall into different categories, sizes, and values. You can always find smaller homes in any neighborhood.

If you want to increase your equity with the help of a low-cost rental than you should opt for low-cost homes. For instance, take a right neighborhood that usually consists of three-bedroom houses that retail for about $75000. In such an area, if you can find one that is worth only $20,000, then it is a good deal. A low-cost house in a great neighborhood is a good bet. This type of home has fantastic potential as a good rental. However, the community you select matters the most. Never underestimate the value of a good area code.

Don't worry even if the rent is slightly low. Ensure that the payments for mortgage, property taxes, as well as maintenance, are paid out of the rental income, and you still have some cash leftover. Keep in mind that the tenants you attract will often be young. A small, low-cost rental is an excellent way to break into the real estate market.

Build Your Team

Real Estate Agent

When there is an economic strain, everyone wants to make responsible choices about where they spend their money. While purchasing a home, every penny matters. Everyone has a specific criterion when it comes to buying a home. Some people want a big house, a swimming pool while some prefer a cozy apartment or loft.

When you're looking for something definitive, it is better to seek help from a professional real estate agent before you go ahead and invest in a property. They know the exact features that will fit your budget and needs. They will also help you out with all the paperwork and assist you throughout the deal. They also know what other properties you could invest in from a business point of view.

A few benefits of seeking advice from real estate agents are as follows.

- They have the right educational background

Real estate agents have the correct knowledge about making and breaking deals. They know the proper procedures and formalities that are necessary for buying and selling properties. They can also give you the essential details and suggest the right properties based on your prerequisites. They also know the local, state, national and international market so they can guide you smoothly.

- Good network and connections

Real estate agents who have been in the market long enough have reliable contacts that provide them the right information. They have connections in the local market as well and know the right places that are available for sale, buying or renting. They will help you to make a profitable decision for your business. They have professional partnerships and contacts in the market and can equip you with a compiled list of references that they have worked with before.

- Help in paperwork

We all know how exhausting the paperwork is when a property has to be sold or bought. Real estate agents have been through this process a lot of times and can help you avoid errors in the paperwork, which will save you a lot of time and money in the future.

- Valuable negotiation skills

Real estate agents will help you to efficiently negotiate the prices and conditions with the other side on your behalf. It saves you the trouble and unnecessary tensions. These brokers have exceptional negotiating and mediating skills. They can marvelously handle situations with a sound mind, and this will prove very beneficial to you.

- Pricing counseling

Real estate agents are very experienced and know the value of the land or property and can make sure that you don't get ripped off and pay the right price. They can help you find the perfect fit for your budget.

Hiring a real estate agent can give you the right idea of what you're in for, and you will get an inside peek at how the business works too.

Property Manager

There are certain things that you should take into consideration for deciding whether you want to hire the services of a property manager or not. For determining this, you can make a list of things that you have got to do, things you cannot do, and the ones that you shouldn't be doing. If property management happens to fall in any of the lists that are mentioned above, then you should hire a property manager.

- Dealing with the complaints from tenants

Who doesn't like the idea of earning passive income from renting out properties? However, this also means that you will have to deal with all the problems and complaints that the tenants might have. By hiring the services of a property manager, you need not worry about it. The property manager will handle all of this for you. Well, your property manager is responsible for taking care of different things like the screening out the tenants. Your property manager should take care of all the time-consuming aspects of finding suitable tenants for your property. You don't have to spend your valuable time on keeping a check on your rental properties. Things like the screening of tenants, any site visits, evictions, and so on should be taken care of by the property manager.

- Focusing on your own business

Take a look at any of the successful real estate moguls, who have managed amass immense wealth. How do you think managed to do all that? Surely, they won't be able to achieve all the success by personally tending to every complaint made by the tenant or by personally fixing the plumbing in each of the properties. They managed to reach the level of success they are at because they knew about the things that they should be spending their time on. If you want your business to grow, then you need to spend considerable time and energy on it; taking care of different properties will eat into your time.

- You cannot possibly be an expert at everything

You certainly cannot know everything. You might be good at a few things, but you certainly cannot do the jobs of a handyman, a plumber, an electrician, a lawyer, an accountant, and other professionals. You are only human, and it is okay if you cannot do all of this. Hire a property manager who has all the necessary contacts for taking care of various problems as and when they arise. The property management company will provide you with every sort of professional service that you might need for the upkeep of the property, and you indeed don't have to wrack your brains for figuring things out. That's a huge burden off your shoulders. It will save you time, energy, and money. You can also get more things done, and you will get better sleep at night knowing that your investments are in safe hands.

- Invest anywhere

Most of the real estate investors tend to have certain self-imposed restrictions regarding investing in other markets. It isn't necessarily bad, but you shouldn't hold your business back from growing. If you have got a good property manager, then there is no reason why you shouldn't live in a different city if you want to. You don't have to drive down for inspecting the property physically. The property manager will do all this for you.

- Best investment decisions

A good property manager will always have your best interest in mind. Before you invest in a property, you can consult your property manager for figuring out whether it is a good investment or not. You can ask them different questions about the neighborhood you are interested in, the vacancy rates, the local market trends, the expected rent on the property, costs of the acquiring the property, getting the potential property thoroughly vetted and so on. Your property manager is your consultant who will help you in taking the best investment decisions.

Hiring a property manager is indeed a good idea. The services they provide outweigh the cost of hiring them.

Be careful while hiring a property manager since the responsibility of taking care of your property rests on them. You need someone who is capable of taking care of your investment and can also develop it further. It will also allow you to concentrate on the other things that require your attention. You can enjoy a steady flow of passive income without having to worry about different issues that keep cropping up with the maintenance of the various properties. If you have got multiple real estate investments, then a property manager will be extremely helpful.

Find the Right Property Manager - Step by Step

Step 1: Get referrals.

The best way to find a trustworthy property manager is by referral. Review the state's Real Estate Commission and the Better Business Bureau to make sure your property manager is licensed and has no grievances against them.

Step 2: Note the first impression.

Put yourself in a potential tenant's place. Would you want to rent a home from this individual?

Step 3: Find out how the individual advertises and manages vacancies.

Ask these questions:

- Where does the property manager advertise vacant homes?
- What kind of signs do they put in front of the property?
- How many vacancies does each property manager have?
- What is the average length of time it takes to place a tenant?

Note: *If the property manager has a website, take a careful look. Is the site outdated? If their website is* *outdated, their business practices might be efficient or effective.*

Step 4: Negotiate the terms of the contract.

Ask these questions:

- How much do you charge for their services? Beware if the fees are too low or high, as this may be a sign that the manager is not experienced or too good to be true.
- How many days notice does the property manager require to terminate the relationship? If you are not satisfied with your property manager's services, it is essential to be able to end their services within 30-60 days, which will give you enough time to find a replacement.

- How are maintenance and repairs handled?

- When should you expect to receive the tenant's rent each month? Is direct deposit an option, or will you receive a check in the mail?

- Will, the property manager, be responsible for keeping the tenant's security deposit, or will you?

- How will the manager deal with a delinquent tenant? What are their eviction proceedings? Ask the manager to describe their process in detail.

Step 5: Examine the property manager's tenant lease agreement.

Ask these questions:

- How much of a security deposit is required of the tenant?

- What is the monthly rent and how long are the lease terms (i.e. months, years)? While you want a good price for your property, if you are charging too much, it will sit empty for a long time.
- How are late rents handled? Is the process clearly written and will a tenant understand the consequences?
- What are the consequences of breaking the lease?

Finding a property manager is not an easy, but dedicating additional energy to this endeavor in the beginning will save you hours of headaches.

Make Your Offer

You like a property that you want to buy, what is the next step? The next step is to make an offer.

The process to make an offer to buy a property can vary from one state to another. In some areas, verbal communication will do, and in others, you need a written agreement. To be on the safe side, it is prudent to make a written agreement. It helps to get rid of all ambiguities and concerns. In case of any legal trouble, you will be safe. The negotiations start when you meet an agent. The agent will ask you questions to gauge your situation and understand the kind of property you need. There will be a lot of phone calls, negotiations, and inspections before you can make an offer.

Ensure that you thoroughly understand the process of the offer. Ask the agent to explain how the process works and check the same with your solicitor. It is a good idea to consult a financial advisor before you decide to invest. Know the price you are willing to pay for the property (the maximum and minimum limits). Remember that it is a negotiation; be prepared for a little haggling. Do plenty of research on the property.

The property should be up to your liking, after all, you will invest a considerable chunk of your finances. Be aware of the seller's motivation to sell, the date of settlement, and any other information that you need. You need to be patient, and this isn't a process that you can complete overnight. Some properties tend to take a while longer than the others. You can ask your solicitor to draw up an agreement of purchase. If the seller offers to do the same, then make sure that your solicitor approves it before you decide to sign anything. Once all the documents are in order, you can approach your financer for their approval to release funds.

Part Two

Become a Landlord

Being a landlord doesn't come cheap. Buying a property to rent out requires serious amounts of money and isn't like buying a smart TV or the latest, top-of-the-line smartphones. It's a very serious investment that involves not only a large number of financial resources but also a serious commitment to making being a landlord worth your while. And what can make it worth your while? On top of the list are the financial benefits.

Financial Benefits

One of the most significant economic benefits of being a landlord is steady and meaningful cash inflows. Many investments can give you meaningful cash inflows, but usually, they're not stable. And while others provide steady cash inflow, they may not necessarily be significant enough to buy you a cup of coffee at Starbucks every day.

But property rental, assuming you do your homework well and can consistently keep your property booked with quality tenants, can provide you with a significant and steady stream of cash in the form of rental income. And this is very helpful when it comes to planning you and your family's finances because it is a very predictable source of income if again; you do your landlord homework very well.

Another financial benefit to being a landlord is being able to lock in your dream home's current price and make it self-liquidating, which means it pays for itself for a period of time until you're financially ready to move in. Some people buy houses in very good areas but are concerned about the affordability based on their current income.

By purchasing their dream home now and renting it out, not only are they able to lock in the current market price and hedge themselves against inflation, but they're also able to pay for part or all of the amortization payments through the rental income the property can generate when leased out. And you can do the same - you can move in when you no longer need to rent out your dream home because either it has been fully paid for by the rental income or your income is already more than sufficient to pay the remaining amortization.

Another financial benefit of being a landlord is a more significant net income after tax. How? Apart from the additional revenue, it can give you via rentals; it will also qualify you for certain tax deductions that you would not be able to enjoy if you're not a registered landlord, mainly depreciation expense. Depreciation is a non-cash expense (doesn't affect your cash flow), but as a tax-deductible expense, it can substantially reduce your taxable income and consequently, your income taxes payable. Think of depreciation as a tax-exempt savings account.

Another financial benefit that's unique to landlords is what's called the 1031 Exchange, which allows you to swap a real property for another - in case you want to dispose of your property in exchange for another later on - without having to pay capital gains taxes from the disposal of such property. What this means is you can sell your rented property and use the proceeds to buy another one and not have to pay capital gains taxes!

Lastly, being a landlord can help you achieve financial leverage. If you buy an investment property on mortgage and rent it out immediately, you can effectively pay way less cash to own that property. How?

Say you bought a $120 thousand-dollar house on a mortgage where your equity or down payment is 30% or $36,000. If you rent out the property at the same amount as your monthly amortization on the mortgage, you're effectively able to own a $120 thousand-dollar property for only $36,000! How cool is that, huh?

The Different Landlord Hats

As a landlord, should you choose to become one, you'd have to take on several different roles and wear different hats. Some of them include:

The Agent Hat

Because you're renting out your property to other people, you'll be the person primarily responsible for looking for quality tenants for your property. Part of your role as a realtor is putting out ads (subject to the Federal Fair Housing Rules), book appointments with prospective tenants, bring them to the property itself for their inspection, and screening your applicants.

The Salesman Hat

Unless you hire a property manager or a broker, you'll have to make the pitch to your prospective tenants to close the deal. You'll have to be aware of the guidelines on "steering" under the Federal Government's Fair Housing Rules, which is applicable when you bring your prospective tenants to your property to show them around it.

The Sherlock Holmes Hat

When selecting the best tenant for your investment property, you'll need to do some detective or private investigator work to gather enough information to help you evaluate your tenant applicants very well and choose the best one. This includes verifying their income and its sources, doing background checks, and running a credit check. Your ability to do this well will determine the quality of your tenant and your overall experience as a landlord.

The Supervisor Hat

It's a bad idea to assume that after signing of the lease contract and once the tenant moves in, you can shift to cruise mode and just let things be. As a landlord, you have both rights and obligations to your tenant, and if you don't keep a right eye on your property and the tenant, it's possible that problems can arise. You'll have to take a proactive approach to both your and the tenants' compliance with the lease contract to minimize any potential issues and problems later on.

The Negotiator Hat

It's not just your potential tenants that you'll have to negotiate with, my friend. You'll also need to negotiate with people who will perform renovation or repair works on your property. Why? So you can get the best price for their services. If you're not able to do this well, it can prevent you from optimizing your rental income due to lower rent or significantly higher renovation or repair expenses.

The Handyman Hat

There will be instances when a maintenance specialist isn't available when urgent repairs need to be done on the property you're leasing out. If you don't know how to perform necessary repairs, you may run into problems with your tenants especially if your tenants are legalistic war-freaks who will pounce on you in the name of their rights as soon as an opportunity presents itself. Being a handyman can go a long way toward minimizing that risk.

The Collector Hat

If you want to ensure you receive the rental payments on time, you'll need to play the role of a collector very well. Let's face it - most people won't pay unless asked. That being said, you'll need to take a pro-active approach to collect your rental income, especially if your tenant starts to become a habitual late payer.

Operating As a Landlord

While being a landlord may appear to be a relatively simple career, it's not. It's not just about buying a property, renting it out, and waiting for it to lay golden eggs that'll automatically come to you. Being a landlord is a business, which makes you officially a small business owner. And being a small business owner, there are many important things you'll need to take care of to optimize revenue and minimize costs.

Why Good Accounting and Records Keeping is Crucial for you as a Landlord.

Accounting and record keeping may be considered as a Batman-and-Robin or Captain America-and-Bucky Barnes duo of being a small business owner. Why? Your ability to maintain proper accounting and other records as a landlord will benefit you in a myriad number of ways:

- It can help you to manage your property rental business better and grow it over time because good records - accounting or otherwise - can help you make much better business, financial and legal decisions.
- It can enable you to keep organized as you deal not just with your tenant but with your service providers or suppliers.
- It can make it much easier for you to always be aware if you're making money in your property rental business.
- It can help you find relevant documents and files more easily when you need them.

- It can help you have an easier time getting a bank loan or take out a mortgage.
- It can help you avoid potential tax problems by helping you accurately check your tax position and pay your taxes on time.
- It can minimize the work your accountant has to do, which can lead to lower fees.
- It can give you a much easier time when filing your taxes.

In short, efficiently keeping accounting and other property rental-related records won't just help you keep things in order, but can help you run your property rental business much more profitable.

Tax Benefits of Being a Landlord

One of the financial benefits I mentioned earlier as a landlord was taxes. In particular, I mentioned about tax-deductions specific to being a landlord. Here are some of those tax deductions, i.e., benefits that you can enjoy as a landlord.

- Mortgage Interest
- Property Taxes
- Landlord Insurance
- Accounting & Bookkeeping
- Repairs
- Depreciation
- Property Management Fees
- Travel
- Home Office & Operating Expenses
- Advertising
- Legal & Support Fees

- Utilities
- Proceeds Are Taxed as Capital Gains if sold after more than one year of ownership.

Compliance with Local, State and Federal Laws

The most important laws you'll need to familiarize yourself with as a landlord are the Federal Government's Fair Housing Laws, in which you'll learn all of your rights and obligations as a landlord. However, you will also need to familiarize yourself with state and local laws that govern property rentals to minimize your risk of getting into legal problems later on. As they say, ignorance of the law excuses no one so you can't use ignorance of laws as an excuse for violating them. This now begs the question, should you hire a lawyer for your property rental business?

To Hire Or Not To Hire A Lawyer?

I suspect that at this point, you only plan to rent one rental property as a newbie landlord while learning the ropes of the business. Or maybe you're thinking of renting out a couple of properties. If so, it may not be practical to hire a lawyer due to apparent financial reasons, i.e., hiring a lawyer is expensive and can eat into your property rental business' bottom line.

The good news is that if you currently don't have plans to operate a property rental conglomerate, you don't have to retain a lawyer. If you just put in enough time to study the basic legal obligations of a landlord under the Fair Housing Laws and your state and local laws, your risks for encountering legal problems can be minimized.

It doesn't mean you should never hire a lawyer ever! There will be legal situations when you must hire a lawyer because such situations can be very sensitive and complicated that you can't afford to make a legal mistake, no matter how small. And what are these situations? These include:

- Audited by the IRS or the State
- Being Investigated or Sued for Illegal Discrimination
- Evicting a Tenant
- Sued for Injury or Illness
- Sued for Major Property Damage.

For situations such as these, which can be very rare if you know your basic obligations as a landlord, you don't have to retain their services indefinitely. Just hire a lawyer as the need arises.

Landlord Insurance

Let's face it - life has a way of throwing unpleasant curveballs at us. And one way to manage those curveballs is through insurance policies. However, getting insurance for your rental property isn't as simple as it seems. Many newbie landlords mistakenly think that a homeowner's insurance policy is sufficient to pay for damages to their rental properties in the event of an accident or a natural disaster. Don't make the same mistake of assuming that the insurance you're getting for your rental property isn't limited to owner-occupied homes only.

This is because insurance on owner-occupied homes will no longer be valid on your home the moment you start leasing it out. Considering that tenants aren't usually held liable under the law for major appliance malfunctions, for injuries suffered while on the property (if not the tenant's fault), or for burglaries, having no adequate insurance means you will shoulder the expenses related to these events being the landlord.

So what type of insurance must you get for your rental property? It's called landlord insurance. This type of policy may come in several different variants, and as such, you must carefully evaluate what your rental property needs by way of protection and use them as a benchmark for choosing the best landlord insurance for your property.

What are the things to look for when shopping for a good landlord insurance policy? There are three important types of protection that your landlord insurance must provide: damages to property, liability protection, and rental default or lost income. And when insurance underwriters give you their proposals, you may see them labeled as DP-1, DP-2 OR DP-3. DP means Dwelling Property and the numbers refer to the levels of coverage provided by the insurance policy, where DP-1 is the lowest level (the bare bones version) and DP-3 being the top-of-the-line and most comprehensive version.

In addition to the three important coverages I mentioned, landlord insurance policies may also feature additional coverage or riders. They're not as crucial as the big 3, but they may prove to be beneficial and help you to save more money over the long term. These include:

- Flood Insurance: Considering the nasty mood Mother Nature is in these days and that most landlord insurance policies don't have flood coverage, this one can be an excellent investment to add in your landlord insurance policy.

- Guaranteed Income Insurance: This rider or coverage helps you protect yourself against losses if your tenant fails to pay his or her rent.
- Emergency Coverage: This coverage will help you cover expenses incurred as a result of emergency repairs or actions that need to be taken on the property, such as when the tenant locks him or herself out of the house and has no spare keys, or when the major water pipe bursts.

Typically, annual owner-occupied home insurance premiums range from $800 to $1,100. But considering the fact that rental properties tend to be at higher risks for incidents and damages, annual premiums on landlord policies may be more expensive by as much as 20%. The length of time for which the property is rented out also affects the insurance premium. Shorter rental periods tend to increase the landlord insurance premiums of a rental property while longer ones tend to reduce it. Why?

This is because tenants who tend to lease properties on a short-term basis have a lower chance of mentioning or noticing maintenance related issues of a property. They can also be more likely to be careless and not understand the layout, the load-bearing capacity, and electrical wirings of the property due to their relatively short stay in it. These increase the risk of damages and for the insurance companies, their chances of paying out claims. To compensate for the higher risks, they'll charge higher premiums.

Finding Tenants

Finding tenants for your rental property isn't as simple or straightforward as it seems. For one, you'll need to be able to put your property out in front of as many qualified potential tenants as possible. For another, you'll also need to convince them that renting your property - at your desired price - will be in their best interests. And lastly, you'll need to be able to do so within the confines of the Federal Government's Fair Housing Laws.

Why you'll need to Understand Fair Housing Laws

Yes, there are rules and regulations that govern your tenant finding activities and violating them can be quite costly. There's a saying in the Bible that "people perish for lack of knowledge." As I wrote earlier, ignorance of the law excuses no one and, as such, ignorance of the law can be very costly. And as a landlord, you'll need to be particularly mindful of the Fair Housing Laws as the most important rules pertaining to your being a landlord is found there. And that includes laws on how to find your tenants.

While the Fair Housing Laws are quite extensive and cover a wide range of topics related to property rentals, you only need to focus on ten things as a landlord. These include Fair Housing Laws on:

- Advertising
- Steering
- Screening Of Applicants
- Occupancy Standards
- Apartment Rules
- Reasonable Accommodation
- Reasonable Modification

- Record Keeping
- Eviction

You can grab your copy of the Fair Housing Laws under the Fair Housing Act at http://www.hud.gov.

Kinds of Advertising for Renting Out Your Property

The primary way you can look for a tenant is via advertisement of your property. Keep in mind that advertising your rental property isn't as simple and straightforward as you think it is. This is one of the important aspects of the Fair Housing Act you'll need to be familiar with because if you advertise in ways that violate the Act, you're screwed even before you start your landlord career.

What does the Act say about how you should advertise your rental property? While it doesn't limit your advertising medium, e.g., print, digital, etc., it does regulate the content of such advertising. Under the law, you should keep your advertisement's content to information that describes the amenities or attributes of your rental property only and don't include information on the personal characteristics of your "dream" tenant. Otherwise, you may be sued for discrimination.

When advertising your rental property, you should stay clear of phrases like:

- "The ideal place for dynamic, young couples" because this can be deemed as discriminating for single people or couples with young children.
- "...in an exclusive part of the Manhattan neighborhood." as this can be construed as only people belonging to a particular economic class are welcome to check out your rental property.
- "The perfect home for Christian/Muslim/Hindu families..." because this can be perceived as religious bigotry.

At the end of your rental property advertisements, you must include a disclaimer such as "The community in which the property is located doesn't discriminate on the basis of nationality, religion, race, color, familial status, disability, or sexual orientation." or the Fair Housing logo. And think twice about including pictures of the property on your advertisements. If you really believe that a picture is needed, do so only after consulting with a lawyer to minimize your legal risks.

Screening Your Tenant Applicants

Your ability to screen your tenant applicants in order to choose the right one for your rental property will determine your overall experience as a landlord. Do it poorly, and you may end up with a tenant straight from the bowels of hell, and if you do it right, you can end up with an angel of a tenant and enjoy a relatively stress-free - and profitable if I may add - stint as a landlord. But this activity is also governed by Fair Housing Laws, so you must know how to do it in accordance with such laws.

As a landlord, you'll need to have a printed or written Tenant Selection Plan that details your criteria for approving tenant applications for your rental property. The selection plan must include guidelines for occupying your property, your policy for the availability of the property, and criterions you will use for accepting tenant applications (these include income, employment history, credit scores, etc.). Also, detailed explanations of each criterion, a general outline of the tenant application process, and a statement that says you adhere to all applicable Fair Housing Laws. And equally important, you must furnish your applicants a copy of your Tenant Selection Plan even before they fill up and sign your rental application forms.

Next, you must also prepare your rental application form. This document is essential because aside from information gathering, it also serves as your official authorization for running background and credit checks later on. Let's talk about information gathering first.

You must not ask your tenant applicants questions about disabilities whether mental or physical. And while you may ask questions concerning lawsuits and substance use (alcohol, drugs, etc.), such questions in the application form must be limited. Perfectly acceptable questions to ask in the application form include those that can help you gather information regarding the applicants' past money judgments, evictions, bankruptcies, and their reasons for leaving their current landlords.

Financial Background Checks

This is probably the most crucial part of screening your tenant applicants. Remember, being a landlord means you're a small business owner and as such, you're in it to make money and not lose it. If you screw up this part of tenant applicant evaluation process, your risk of ending up with a delinquent, non-paying tenant increases substantially. Worse, you might even end up with a money laundering or criminal tenant, which will not only be a financial problem but a huge legal one too. But you must do this right, i.e., in compliance with Fair Housing Laws.

Before even running any checks, you must remember to have them fill up and sign your rental application form first, which should include a clause that authorizes you to run background, financial, and credit checks on the applicants. If you conduct credit or background checks without any authorization, you can face serious legal problems. So do it right the first time by having them fill up and sign your rental application form first before running checks on them.

There are three critical steps to verifying your tenant applicants' income or financial capacity: Securing vital financial documents, verifying employment with the employer (if employed), and running a credit check.

<u>Securing Financial Documents</u>

The first process of evaluating your prospective tenants' financial capacity is to ask for copies of key financial documents from them, such as last three months' bank statements (if self-employed), their W2 forms, and last three months' pay-slips (if employed). You will also need to request a copy of the prospective tenants' Form 4506-T form IRS, which is practical but equally effective as Form 4506.

Employment Verification

If your prospective tenant is an employee, another step needs to be taken, which is to make sure that he or she's really working for the employer indicated on the application form. For this, you can go straight to their employer considering the signed application form includes authorization to conduct background checks, including employment. If for some reason the employer refuses to divulge information on the grounds that they don't know if you're authorized to do so, you can either ask the applicant to call them and vouch for you or show them a copy of the signed rental application form that includes your authorization.

Credit Checks

This final step will help give you an idea of your prospective tenants' true financial condition and capacity, which can go a long way towards helping your protect your rental property and successfully make money off it. Applicants with very good credit scores (excellent credit history, timely payment of bills) have much lower risks of not being able to pay rent than those with low scores.

A credit check will give you information that can help you get an excellent estimate if an applicant is able to pay the monthly rent on time or not successfully. Some of the information included in a credit check - which may vary according to the agency hired - include:

- Confirmed personal details such as full name, addresses (both current and past), birthday, employers (current and past), spouse's identity, and social security number
- Credit history including outstanding loans (including the type of loans, amount of loans, available credit limit, the age of loans, last two years' payment history, co-borrowers if any), credit card accounts, and bank accounts
- Public records such as financial judgments and tax liens vs. the applicants, bankruptcies filed, and reported evictions
- The names of people or institutions that have asked for a credit report on the applicants within the last 12 months

- For some reports, even the applicant's credit or FICO score may be included.

Information Needed For a Credit Check

To successfully conduct a credit check, you must know the applicant's full name, birthday, address in the last two years, social security number, current employer (if employed), and current or most recent landlord. And as mentioned earlier, you'll need to be authorized to run the check, which should already be included in the signed rental application form submitted to you.

Turning Down an Applicant, Legally

It's in your best interests to accept an applicant that meets your criteria, which should've been documented and given to your applicants before even filling up and signing an application form. But as the Highlander movie and television series always says, there can only be one approved tenant per property. This means you'll have to turn applicants down along the way. But the way you turn down applicants must also be compliant with Fair Housing laws. Otherwise, you're putting yourself at risk of being sued for "discrimination."

To avoid being sued for perceived discrimination, you shouldn't just tell your rental applicants that they didn't make the cut without giving them reasons why you're not renting the property out to them, even if you actually have legal reasons for doing so. Legal reasons that are not communicated won't cut it for you-you'll need to communicate it to them when you formally inform them of your decision to turn down their applications. And under the Fair Housing Act, you may not turn down rental applicants on the basis of nationality, skin color, disabilities, marital status, gender, religion or race.

You may turn down rental applicants for as long as you can prove that all applicants were evaluated equally and using the same criteria and process, and your basis for doing so should be a high probability that they won't be able to pay rent (based on financial records and credit checks) or if the rental applicants can pose serious security threats to the property and the neighborhood in which it's located. But even if you have the legal justification to turn applicants down, you must do it the "right" way too, especially if the basis for doing so are credit check results or other public records.

If your basis for turning down a rental applicant is because of unfavorable results of conducted credit checks, you must give the applicant an Adverse Action Notice, which is a federal requirement under Federal Fair Credit Reporting Act. This document tells the applicant that the application was turned down because of adverse findings or results of the credit check conducted on him or her. The contact details of the agency that ran the check must also be included in the notice to give the applicant the chance to access the report and if ever, contest it.

If the applicant responds to your notice saying that the credit check's information is not accurate, you can ask the person to contact the agency that prepared the report directly to contest the information. This is because you have no authority and basis for determining whether or not the information on the report is inaccurate, as well as to revise the report. It's your legal right to insist that in the absence of any revision, clarification or adjustment in the credit report prepared by the agency you hired, your decision stands.

If you turn down an applicant because of a dangerous criminal record, keep in mind that the records must show that the applicant has been convicted of dangerous crimes that can potentially put the property and the people living within the area at risk. Merely being arrested won't cut it when it comes to determining the qualifications of a rental applicant. Other restrictions per the United States Department of Housing And Urban Development:

- You can't use blanket statements or terms in your Tenant Selection Plan that says something like "applicants with criminal convictions will be turned down or rejected." because it's considered as a violation of the Fair Housing Act's provisions on discrimination.

- You must provide the applicant with a denial letter as well as instructions on how he or she can secure a copy of the report. Or record that you used as the basis for turning down the application if such information or record was the basis for your decision (the law doesn't require you to provide a copy of the report to the applicant).

To have a much easier time when it comes to rejecting rental applications correctly, the United States Land Protection Agency suggests that you make a standardized letter that you can give to rejected applicants, which contain a checklist of possible legal reasons for rejecting a rental applicant. As a landlord, you merely check the reason on the list for your decision to turn down an application. These reasons should include:

- Unacceptable rental offer price
- Inadequate income
- Inability to verify employment
- Poor credit history (if this is the reason, attach an adverse action letter)
- Pets
- Smoking
- The applicant provided false information on the application form
- Incomplete information on the application form
- Others

Having such a standardized letter already prepared can help you turn down rental applicants in a more time efficient manner because with a template on hand, you won't have to spend so much time crafting letters individually and responding to the complaints of rejected applicants. More importantly, such a letter provides the rejected applicants a proper and comprehensive explanation for the rejection.

Lastly, you have to remember that when it comes to approving rental applications for your property, you must do so on a first-come-first-served basis. And by this, the law doesn't mean the first applicant always wins. By first, the law means to say that the first qualified applicant. Even if an applicant was first in line, but it was proven that he or she's not qualified, his or her application can be rejected. Tell the rental applicant the real reason for them being denied, i.e., that even though they were approved or qualified to rent your property, someone else beat them to the draw by virtue of being first in line. If you have other rental properties, you can tell them to apply for those if they're interested.

Keep these in mind when you have to turn down your rental property's applicants. By keeping within these parameters and complying with legal requirements for doing so, you'll be able to protect yourself from the hassles of having to address discrimination claims against you.

Accepting Tenants

As mentioned earlier, the first QUALIFIED rental applicant or the first approved rental applicant is the one that should be accepted. And to avoid discrimination claims from disgruntled applicants, you should have a system for documenting receipt of an application and for objectively establishing who the first qualified rental applicant is.

An excellent way to do this is by through time stamping and providing the rental applicants with a time-stamped, photocopied version of their signed application forms. The time stamping establishes the date and time of the application form's submission while the duplicate copy, which must be timestamped as well and signed as received by you, gives them a hard copy or evidence that they filed their application at a specific date and time - a sign of goodwill if you may.

Another purpose for their copies of the application forms is leverage when a discrimination claim arises. When you give them the copy, you can ask them if the date and time of receipt stamped on their copies are accurate. So if they claim that they submitted it earlier, you can always refer to the fact that they confirmed the accuracy of the time stamp when they submitted the application form. It's an excellent way to protect yourself against rental applicants who have serious attitude problems.

Once you have chosen "the one," you'll need to prepare the lease contract, the details of which we'll discuss in the next session.

The Landlord-Tenant Relationship

After notifying "the one" that his or her application was approved, you need to familiarize yourself with your end of the bargain, i.e., your responsibilities and obligations as a landlord. While there are many of them and the laws governing the landlord-tenant relationship may vary, what's important is to know the most basic ones, which will be enough to make sure you avoid legal problems down the line.

Landlord Obligations under the Law

These are 5 of the most important duties of a landlord under the landlord-tenant law:

- Security Deposit
- Disclosure of Owner
- Delivering Possession of the Unit
- Maintenance

- Liability.

Security Deposit

As a landlord, you have the right to ask for prepaid rent or a security deposit to protect yourself against non-payment of rent. But with such a right comes an obligation, which is to manage that prepaid rent or security deposit. This is because the security deposit or prepaid rent isn't really yours, to begin with. It's just given to you as a precaution against non-payment, which means it'll only be yours once the tenant defaults on his or her rental payments to you or other breaches that require monetary compensation based on the lease contract.

As a landlord, you will also be obligated to comply with various local and state laws on rental security deposits such as maximum amount of security deposit asked from tenants, where to keep the security deposit, return of the deposit, and how to dispose of the security deposit in case you sell your rental property during the term of the lease.

Disclosure of Owner

Whoever signs the lease contract on your behalf - whether it's you or an authorized agent - the obligation to disclose to the tenant important information on the real owner of the property, which in this case is you. So what are the things you'll need to tell the tenant? Your complete name, address, and the names and addresses of the people you have authorized to manage the property on your behalf including making repairs and collect rent, address complaints and give notices if any.

How should you disclose such information? First, it has to be in writing.

You should sign it and prepare a duplicate copy, which will serve as your receiving copy and evidence that you have disclosed such information. Second, you'll need to give the information to the tenant before his or her tenancy starts. In case there are changes to the information while the tenant is in the middle of tenancy, you must immediately notify him or her of the changes, also in writing.

Why do you need to do this? First of all, it's required by the landlord-tenant law. But more importantly, it can also safeguard both you and the tenant from legal problems during a tenancy. By providing such information to your tenant, he or she knows who to get in touch with for any concerns related to the property as well as who are authorized to receive their rental payments apart from you. In the event you're not able to disclose this information to the tenant, then the default contact or go-to person for all matters pertaining to the property is the person who collects the rent.

Deliver Possession of the Property

Another obligation of a landlord is delivery of possession of the property to your approved rental applicant. What this means is you must ensure that the property in question is vacant and ready to be moved into by the tenant at the date indicated in your lease contract. If you're not careful to make the unit available on that date, you can face legal problems if the tenant decides to take you to court on account of your inability to fulfill your end of the bargain.

If there are illegal occupants in the property in question, you as a landlord have the right to pursue legal action to have such occupants evicted and to receive damages as a result of your inability to have the property rented out on account of the illegal occupation of such property.

Maintenance of the Property

As a landlord, it's your legal responsibility to keep the rental property in good and livable condition, i.e., this means keeping it habitable, safe, and clean. This also means you must comply with all building codes, maintain the property's common areas (if any), keep vital utilities in good working condition (e.g., plumbing, water supply, heat, electricity), and provide a good trash disposal facility.

Limited Liability Obligations

As a landlord, you're generally obligated to comply fully with the landlord-tenant law, which includes complying with the terms and conditions specified in your lease contract with the tenant. In many states, however, you may be set free from these obligations the moment you sell your property and have properly notified the tenant that the property has a new manager or owner. At this point, your obligations under the landlord-tenant law and lease contract are transferred to the new owner. But being the landlord who collected the rental deposit, you are still under obligation to manage the security deposit given by the tenant. For this, you have two possible courses of action. The first is you can transfer the security deposit to the property's new owner, less any deductions allowed under the lease contract, and give the tenant a written notice that you have given the security deposit to the new owner. Doing so will relieve you of the obligation of managing the security deposit.

The other option is to give the deposit back to the tenant, minus any deductions allowed under the contract.

Finally, you must check local and state laws that pertain to landlord-tenant relationships to make sure you don't fail to fulfill your legal obligations as a landlord.

Obligations and Responsibilities of the Tenant

Relationships are a two-way thing, and this includes your relationship with your tenant. As such, your tenant also has his or her own set of obligations under the landlord-tenant law, some of which may vary depending on local or state laws that govern such a relationship. Make sure that your tenant is aware of their obligations under the law to minimize the risk of problems with the lease later on.

Generally speaking, a tenant has three general obligations: to comply with the lease agreement or contract, to maintain the property's premises, and to allow you - the landlord - to go inside the property.

Compliance with the Lease Contract

By affixing his or her signature on the lease contract or agreement, the tenant agrees to comply with all the terms, conditions, and provisions of the contract. Lease contracts come in different forms and lengths - some can be as short as a page while others may be more than ten pages long. The important things are that your lease contract's terms and conditions must not violate any Federal, state, or local laws.

What should your lease contract include? While the number of items you can put in your lease contract is practically endless, there are only a few that are considered to be essential or crucial. These include:

- Duration of the lease, with an exact date for the lease contract's expiration and move-out dates
- Proper use of the property, i.e., do's and don'ts
- Terms and conditions for handling the security deposit
- The amount of monthly rental to be paid, how payment is to be made, and dates for rental payments
- Courses of action for late or non-payment of rent, including the amount of penalties and charges to be levied
- Requirements and procedures for moving out
- Disclosure on use of lead-based paints.

Maintenance of the Property's Premises

Aside from the obligations specified in the lease contract, your tenant is also obligated to maintain the property's premises properly. These obligations include:

- Complying with housing and building codes, particularly those that apply to tenants that usually focus on health and safety standards
- Safe and sanitary maintenance of the property, which means that your tenant should keep the property in a clean and reasonably safe condition
- Clean, safe, and proper garbage disposal, i.e., not letting garbage and other wastes to build up inside the property
- Keeping plumbing facilities such as the showers, toilets, and faucets in clean working condition
- Proper use of all electricity and plumbing facilities, i.e., operating cooling, heating, plumbing, and

electrical facilities in accordance with their intended uses only

- Proper use and maintenance of appliances that you supplied in the property
- Preventing damages to the property, except for normal wear and tear
- Respecting the neighbors' right to peace and quiet, i.e., not playing loud music or letting children run and shout wildly around the property
- Prohibiting the use of controlled or illegal substances in the property
- Leaving the smoke detectors untouched
- Leaving the paint job alone especially for homes built prior to 1978, which are highly likely to contain lead and other hazardous materials (if paint jobs

are needed, the tenant must inform you first)

- Keep molds from growing in the property and in the event of mold growth and notify you immediately if there are molds growing in the property.

Allow You to Enter the Property

You as a landlord have the right to enter the property being leased. It is important for you to understand that you are more than just the owner of the property, you have the legal obligation to maintain its safe and proper condition. But this isn't a blanket authority to just barge into the property at any time you deem fit.

Under the law, you may only do so during reasonable hours. While the definition of reasonable hours may vary across different states, it's customarily considered as normal business hours, i.e., between 9 in the morning to 6 in the afternoon. However, reasonable hours may also include times of the day or night that fall outside the 9-6 window such as during emergency situations (gas leaks, fire, flooding), or when the tenant requests for an urgent repair in the property. You'd also need to provide the tenant with at least 24 hours prior notice before entering the property regardless of the reason for going inside. The need for notice can only be discarded under the following situations:

- Emergencies
- Maintenance works that have been scheduled beforehand and in the lease contract
- Violations of health and safety laws
- Abandoned property
- Order of the Court

Lastly, the tenant can't just change the locks on the property's doors without your consent as a landlord. And in the event that you permit the tenant to do so, the tenant is obligated to give you your own set of keys to the new doors/locks.

Enforcing the Lease Contract

Equally important as having an iron-clad lease contract is the proper enforcement of such a contract. Unless enforced, a lease contract is practically worthless. And enforcing the contract begins even before the contract is signed. You can already start enforcing the contract as soon as tenants apply to rent your property, i.e., inform them of all your requirements for renting the property through your advertising, marketing, and your rental application forms.

To be specific, you must inform them of your credit, income, and other rental requirements in very clear terms in your rental application forms. Doing so will help your rental applicants know right off the bat if they have what it takes to be approved and if they can quickly comply with your requirements should they be approved. At this stage, you can already minimize your risks for non-compliance by filtering the rental applicants at the onset.

After performing due diligence and approving a rental applicant, the next step to enforcing the lease contract is to prepare a lease contract and have it signed by both you and the tenant. Make sure that your lease contract - at a minimum - includes the terms I enumerated earlier in this chapter to make sure you have the most important bases covered.

During the lease signing, don't just give the tenant the lease contract for signing. Take your time to explain each and every section of the lease contract so that they know what they're getting into. And if it's alright with the tenant, video the whole thing so you'll have documentary evidence that you have explained the provisions of the lease contract to the tenant in detail and that he or she has expressed to you that the provisions were understood.

Lastly, regular inspection of the property - in accordance with the law and with the lease contract's provisions - will help you nip potential problems in the bud. It's much easier to ensure compliance with regular visits or inspections because you can already inform the tenant if he or she's violating any of the lease contract's provisions and by doing so, you give them the chance to comply immediately. It can be much harder to enforce compliance if the tenant has been doing something that violates the contract for a long time already.

Evicting Tenants

In a perfect world, all tenants comply with each and every iota of their lease contract. In such a world, there's no need to kick tenants out before the end of the contract but unfortunately, we live in an imperfect world and as such, there's is a chance that you'll have to evict a tenant as your final course of action in response to continuous violations of your lease contract. In the event, you'll have to resort to this, keep in mind the following important things about evicting your tenant.

State Eviction Laws

You'll have to remember that laws governing the eviction of tenants vary across different states throughout the country and as such, it'll be in your best interests to understand and consider your property's state-specific eviction laws as you craft your lease contract. That way, you can ensure that your lease contract will have the necessary legal bite to be enforced and to let your tenant know that he or she shouldn't take his or her obligations under the contract lightly.

The Landlord-Tenant Law

Most of the states - at least 21 of them - have based their specific landlord-tenant laws on the Uniform Residential Landlord and Tenant Act or URLTA, which provides a very detailed description of how to legally evict a tenant. By familiarizing yourself with the URLTA, you are in an excellent position to handle the eviction process in the most efficient way that's legally possible.

Don't DIY It

In most cases, self-help approaches can be very effective. Evicting tenants isn't one of them. In fact, all states prohibit evicting clients using a DIY approach. Even if your tenant is one that seems to have been puked out from the bowels of hell and is already damaging your property, you're still not allowed to take matters into your own hands by:

- Physically moving your tenant's things out of the property
- Physically removing your tenant from the property, e.g., injecting a sedative and dragging him or her out of your property
- Change the locks of the property to prevent him or her from entering the property
- Cut off crucial utilities such as water, gas, and electricity

- Do things that will make the property uninhabitable like dumping a truckload of manure in the front yard.

If you want the court to side with you, make sure to follow the law. By adhering to laws and with your tenant from hell blatantly violating them, it's almost a sure thing that the court will decide in your favor - and fast.

Make It Valid

Don't undertake an eviction process without ensuring that you have a legal and valid basis for doing so. Some of the best and most valid (not to mention legal) reasons to have a tenant evicted include failure to pay rent, non-compliance with the provisions of the lease contract, severely damaging the property, violating local ordinances (health, occupancy, and noise), and putting the health and safety of other occupants and neighbors in jeopardy. Remember, the adage "innocent until proven guilty" holds true in the eviction process so make sure you can provide documented evidence against the tenant you plan to evict.

A Formal Eviction Notice

Once you've clearly established and documented your tenant's continued violation of the provisions of your lease contract or of local noise, occupancy, and health ordinances, it's time to get the eviction ball rolling by giving your tenant an adequate eviction notice, which is a written document that tells your tenant that you're evicting him or her, why you're evicting him or her, and the things he or she can do to prevent the eviction from being carried out like paying their arrears.

What makes for an adequate eviction notice? It must include a deadline for compliance or moving out and the amount owed (if it's about rent payment arrears, including penalties and charges), it must be posted on the property's front door and sent via registered mail through the United States Postal Service, and it must be posted with a specific number of days prior to filing an eviction case with the local courts. At this point, the ball is already in their court.

File With the Local Courts and Attend Court-Scheduled Hearings

After several days have passed (check with your local and state laws as to the requirement) and the tenant continues to be unrepentant, it's time to file an eviction case with the local courts that have jurisdiction over the property. Provide documentary evidence proving that you had complied with eviction laws by giving the tenant ample time after serving the notice before you filed the case, such as a receipt from registered mail to minimize any problems with your case. After you have filed the case, the court will send a summons to your tenant to notify him, or her of the eviction case filed.

If the case proceeds without the tenant doing anything to comply with your lease contract, court hearings will be held where both you and the tenant will be given a chance to present your cases. Attendance in these hearings is mandatory so make sure to clear your schedule to attend these. When you attend these hearings, make sure you're well prepared to establish your position on the matter by preparing the following documents on hand as evidence that the tenant deserves to be evicted under the law:

- A copy of the signed lease contract
- Returned checks (if any)

- Payment records
- Documented communications between you and the tenant
- A copy of the eviction notice you gave to the tenant
- Proof that the tenant received the eviction notice, e.g., a signed receiving copy of the notice or receipt of registered mail from the US Postal Service.

The single biggest potential area of contention that the tenant can use to wiggle out of the eviction case is that he or she wasn't adequately informed. That's why having a documented proof of receipt is essential. Payment records are tough to fake or manipulate, but it's very easy to cast doubts on your informing them properly of the eviction if you don't have documentary evidence of them receiving the notice.

Eviction

If you do your homework very well, there shouldn't be any reason for the courts to deny you of the right to evict the tenant. It'll just be a matter of "when" and not "if." Once the court has decided in your favor, the tenant will be given anywhere from 2 to 7 days to vacate the property, which will depend on where the property is located.

You may be asking, what if the tenant doesn't leave within the deadline set by the court? At that point, you're still not allowed to physically remove the tenant and his or her stuff out of the property by yourself. You'll need to get somebody from the Sheriff's department to do it for you. Leave the physical removal of the tenant to the local government to avoid any chances of the tenant being able to sue you for damages.

Hiring a Property Manager

After reading through the previous sessions, you might think the hassles seem to outweigh the financial benefits of being a landlord. And I don't blame you for it, especially if you're relatively new to the industry. But there is a way for you to be a landlord without the perceived "hassles": hire a property manager.

Distance

The distance between your place of residence and your rental property is one of the most important factors to consider when hiring a property manager, regardless if you own one. It's very tempting to believe that going back and forth to your property just a few times a year or your capacity to go to the property with very little notice would be more than enough to stay updated with potential issues related to managing your rental property. But believe me, it isn't. This is because potential problems related to your tenants and the rental property aren't predictable, i.e., they don't have a fixed schedule.

If your rental property's just a few blocks away from your home, maybe distance wouldn't be a problem. But if it's several hours away, then it could be. Hiring a property manager located near your rental property can help you mitigate this issue.

Experience

Managing a property requires expertise, time, and to some extent, hard work. If you're a newbie, which I suspect you are, the chances are that you don't have any experience managing a rental property yet. While you can try to wing it at first, doing so puts you at high risk of running into serious legal problems because the property rental laws - at least in the United States - are very specific, thorough, and strict with potentially severe ramifications if violated.

Professional property managers can provide the necessary experience, time, and work that will let you manage your rental property in accordance with the laws of the country, state, and city. This can help you buy enough time to learn the ropes of the business so that when the time comes, you can do it on your own should you choose to do so.

The Property's Condition upon Purchase

The condition of the property you will purchase for the purpose of renting out will determine the amount of work you'll have to put into it in terms of sprucing it up to attract potential tenants and maintaining it. The more depreciated the property is, the more work you'll need to put in and vice versa.

Unless you're loaded enough to buy a property that's in remarkably pristine condition, the chances are high that you'll only be able to afford to buy a rental property that requires repairs and renovations to be attractive to potential quality tenants. That being said, hiring a property manager can relieve you of the heavy burden of having to conduct repair and maintenance works on your rental property. And as your property rental business grows and expands to include even more properties, the work needed to manage it will also grow by leaps and bounds. With a reliable property manager, you need not worry about that.

Screening of Tenants

As a landlord, you must be able to effectively screen your tenant applicants because as I've written earlier, it will determine your overall experience as a landlord. If a tenant from the bowels of hell is able to slip through the cracks and get approved, you may regret having become a landlord in the first place. Tenant screening is one of those aspects of property rental that you shouldn't take for granted.

Property managers are trained in all facets of property management, including the screening of tenant applicants. The outstanding ones are able to smell bad tenants from a mile away, and more importantly, they know how to go about advertising and to market the property so that only desirable tenants are most likely to apply and they can do so within the boundaries of the Fair

Housing Act. By hiring a property manager, you can significantly increase your chances of being able to attract the right kind of tenant and experience property rental heaven here on earth.

Time

Time is a precious commodity that all people have equal amounts of every day, regardless of social status or race. That makes time the most precious commodity of all - it's something you can't take back once lost. And hiring a property manager gives you the luxury of extra time for what's more important in your life.

This can be more important if you have a full-time day job, which can eat up the majority of your waking hours, and if you have a family. Unless you hire a property manager to manage your rental property, there's a pretty good chance that you'll have less time for the things that matter most to you such as family, friends, church, or your "me" time.

How to Choose a Property Manager

Considering the sensitive nature of the job, you must choose your property manager wisely. So how do you go about doing it? Here are some tips to help you do that.

Referrals

This is the best way to go about it. With referrals, especially from people you trust, you can skip the trial-and-error approach to selecting the right property manager. When someone refers a property manager to you, ask why that person highly recommends him or her. Sometimes, what's "good" for some may not be for others so by asking for details on the reasons for their referral, you can evaluate whether or not to hire that referred property manager.

Search Online

If you don't know anybody who can refer a good property manager to you, don't fret. You can search for one online via reputable websites such as http://www.simplifyem.com/property-management and https://www.allpropertymanagement.com/.

Consider Several Property Managers

Don't just consider one property manager candidate, interview several. By considering more than just one, you'll be able to sift the potentially good ones from the bad by simple comparison. Often times, it's hard to evaluate whether or not somebody is on top of their game without others to compare them to. By interviewing several managers, you'll be able to get an idea of what's good or bad and what's realistic or not when it comes to property management services. And competition among your property manager candidates can also help you get a lower price for the same quality of service.

It's Worth the Price Tag

Managing a rental property requires a high level of expertise and experience in the industry. As a newbie, you don't have those luxuries, and if you go at it alone, it's possible that you might inadvertently break a couple of Fair Housing and Landlord-Tenant laws along the way, which may prove to be costly financially and legally. That's why getting the services of a property manager is crucial, at least for the first few years of your property rental business. It will allow you to do things right while buying you enough time to learn how to do it yourself.

Eventually, you can choose to end the property manager's services and manage your rental properties on your own if you believe you have the necessary expertise and experience already. Or you can choose to continue hiring one and enjoy the fruits of your property rental business more.

Conclusion

I would like to thank you once again for purchasing this book. I hope this book was an informative read.

By now, you must be tempted by the concept of rental property investing. One of the best real estate investments that you can make is to invest in a rental property. Maybe you want to invest in rental properties to save for your retirement, supplement your income, or for any other reason. Regardless of your reason, rental property investments are quite lucrative. With the help of the information provided in this book, you can make an informed decision. You no longer have to run around from one source to the other to gather information about rental property investing. Everything you need to know is present within the pages of this book. So, what are you waiting for?

All that is left for you to do is get started today! All the best for your future investments!

Famous Quotes About Real Estate

Here a collection of classic and famous real estate quotes from thought leaders and personalities to keep you motivated, while giving you excellent insights into the business and the value of owning a property.

"Real estate cannot be lost or stolen, nor can it be carried away. Purchased with common sense, paid for in full, and managed with reasonable care, it is about the safest investment in the world." - **Franklin D. Roosevelt**

"This is a real-estate-driven economy from top to bottom." - **Christopher Thornberg**

"If you don't own a home, buy one. If you own a home, buy another one. If you own two homes, buy a third. And, lend your relatives the money to buy a home." - **John Paulson, investor and multi-billionaire**

"Owning a home is a keystone of wealth… both financial affluence and emotional security" - **Suze Orman**

"Real estate is an imperishable asset, ever increasing in value. It is the most solid security that human ingenuity has devised. It is the basis of all security and about the only indestructible security." - Russell Sage, **American Financier and Politician**

"Land monopoly is not only monopoly, but it is by far the greatest of monopolies; it is a perpetual monopoly, and it is the mother of all other forms of monopoly." - **Winston Churchill**

"The smallest patch of green to arrest the monotony of asphalt and concrete is as important to the value of real estate as streets, sewers and convenient shopping." - **James Felt, New York Times**

*"In any market, in any country, there are developers who make money. So I say all of this doom and

gloom, but there will always be people who make money, because people always want homes." - **Sarah Beeny**

"As soon as the land of any country has all become private property, the landlords, like all other men, love to reap where they never sowed, and demand a rent even for its natural produce." - **Adam Smith, Wealth of Nations**

"The right to private property meant at the same time the right and duty to be personally concerned about your own well-being, to be personally concerned about your family's income, to be personally concerned about your future. This is hard work." - **Mikhail Khodorkovsky**

"There have been few things in my life which have had a more genial effect on my mind than the possession of a piece of land." - **Harriet Martineau**

"Before you start trying to work out which direction the property market is headed, you should be aware that there are markets within markets." - **Paul Clitheroe**

"If you do not like real estate, all you have to do is make hamburgers, build a business around that hamburger, and franchise it." - **Robert Kiyosaki**

"The major fortunes in America have been made in land." - **John D. Rockefeller**

"Markets always change, and as soon as there's downturn, cleanliness becomes a major value." - **Donald Trump**

"Look at market fluctuations as your friend rather than your enemy; profit from folly rather than participate in it." - **Warren Buffet**

"It's tangible, it's solid, it's beautiful. It's artistic, from my standpoint, and I just love real estate." - **Donald Trump**

"Every day, you'll have opportunities to take chances and to work outside your safety net. Sure, it's a lot easier to stay in your comfort zone… in my case, business suits and real estate… but sometimes you have to take risks. When the risks pay off, that's when you reap the biggest rewards." - **Donald Trump**

"Now, one thing I tell everyone is learn about real estate. Repeat after me: real estate provides the highest returns, the greatest values and the least risk. " - **Armstrong Williams**

"He is not a full man who does not own a piece of land." - **Hebrew Proverb**

"Buy real estate in areas where the path exists and buy more real estate where there is no path, but you can create your own." - **David Waronker, American real estate investor**

"I made a tremendous amount of money on real estate. I'll take real estate rather than go to Wall Street and get 2.8 percent. Forget about it." - **Ivanka Trump**

"Ninety percent of all millionaires become so through owning real estate. More money has been made in real estate than in all industrial investments combined. The wise young man or wage earner of today invests his money in real estate." - **Andrew Carnegie, Scottish businessman and philanthropist**

"Buying real estate is not only the best way, the quickest way, the safest way, but the only way to become wealthy." - **Marshall Field**

"Landlords grow rich in their sleep without working, risking or economising." - **John Stuart Mill, English philosopher and economist**

"The best investment on earth is earth." - **Louis Glickman**

CAN YOU DO ME A FAVOR?

If you enjoyed this book, would you take a few moments and write a review on Amazon? A short review will help, and it would mean a lot to me.

If you know someone who is thinking about buying their first real estate property, please send him or her a copy of this book.

Acknowledgments

A special thanks to my precious wife (Ashley) who has loved me and encouraged me throughout this process. I am grateful for the support I have received during the development of this book. You have touched and marked my life far beyond words.

A special appreciation to my employees who journeyed with me on my book publishing adventure. Thank you for motivating me to keep writing.

ABOUT THE AUTHOR

Lawrence Anthony is an award-winning real estate investor and entrepreneur. He is best known for creating his real estate portfolio of single-family homes with no-money-down. Lawrence is the founder of Warrick Estates and Investments and now mentoring other aspiring investors. He is passionate about researching and then sharing the most important information about real estate, market cycles, raising capital, and the economy.

NOTES

www.ingramcontent.com/pod-product-compliance
Lightning Source LLC
Chambersburg PA
CBHW031629210526
45464CB00004B/1808